Autumn Seele.. ..u

cat, Meena. Th .... puonsned work.

This book is dedicated to my sister, Megan, who always believed in me and my dreams.

Autumn Seeley

PINS AND ROSES

AUSTIN MACAULEY PUBLISHERS™

LONDON • CAMBRIDGE • NEW YORK • SHARJAH

Ordering Information
Quantity sales: Special discounts are available on quantity purchases by corporations, associations, and others. For details, contact the publisher at the address below.

Publisher's Cataloging-in-Publication data
Seeley, Autumn
Pins and Roses

ISBN 9781685621827 (Paperback)
ISBN 9781685621841 (ePub e-book)
ISBN 9781685621834 (Audiobook

Library of Congress Control Number: 2023908660

www.austinmacauley.com/us

First Published 2023
Austin Macauley Publishers LLC
40 Wall Street, 33rd Floor, Suite 3302
New York, NY 10005
USA

mail-usa@austinmacauley.com
+1 (646) 5125767

I pictured my future
It was blue and by the ocean
Sea salt and sand spilling between my fingers
Ran my hands through your hair
I whispered I love you
The ocean screamed it back
As it swallowed you into the blue

I'm not encouraging your self-isolation
But break your own heart for once
Just to know what it feels like to be in control
Even if it's just for a moment

If pins and roses scattered the floor
And I stood barefoot across the room
You would tell me to come to you
And I would
Bleeding ruby behind me
Just to take you in my arms and stain your shirt with tears
So you may look at my bleeding soles with disgust

Sometimes,
I am unsure if I miss you at all
Or if I simply miss the feeling of feeling complete

The next time you go to tell me that you love me,
I hope the words become stuck in your throat
So you can fucking choke

I've had lovers stay the night and last a lifetime
And I've had soulmates stay by me for years only to forget
me in the morning
Believe me when I say
Time means nothing and never has

I told you I was fire
So you touched my skin and burned for me

I told you I loved you
So you asked me if I'd do anything for you
And when I told you I would, you asked me to love myself
as much as I love you

Maybe I don't love you after all

When I think of home, I don't think of a house
I don't think of warm beds and running baths
When I think of home, I think of coming to pieces in your
arms
When I think of home, I always think of you

I wonder if I'll ever be back home again

You told me you were thirsty
So I let you drink from my stream
You told me you were hungry
So I let you eat from my garden
You told me you were tired
So I let you sleep in my bed
You told me that you loved me
So I let you stay with me
But you found clearer streams
Sweeter fruit
And suddenly,
You didn't love me anymore

Fate never gave me a damned chance
She spun me out of her arms and into yours
So we danced until we wore holes in the soles of our shoes
And when I grew too heavy on your arm,
Fate pulled me back to her
And she's been spinning me around in circles ever since

I'll love you one minute for every star in the sky
And when infinity collapses around us,
I'll love you till the air leaves my lungs and my heart goes
to piece
From then,
I'll love you evermore

All my life, I've wanted to be a flower
Bursting through the cracks of the sidewalk
Something beautiful amongst the desolate
As time has gone on, I've accepted that I have become the
desolate
The crack along the sidewalk
And so I wait for the flower to bloom within me
However long it may take

You were an acquired taste
I didn't have the patience

I'm sorry I couldn't stomach you

I still remember you

Often

Always

But never with the same romantic notion I used to

When he kisses me, he is soft

Sweet

Patient

And I remember how you were

Brash

Smoldering

Impatient

His hands are warm

Gentle

He understands me

And I remember how you were

Cold

With no interest in the temperament of the seas you parted

The day I forget you will be the day I am free

There are parts of me I have not touched for years
If the light finally parted the darkness, you would see more
than you could handle
And I believe that you believe you want to know me
To love me in my entirety
But I don't think that you could

Sometimes
I don't think anyone could

I think of your mess
The way your lips parted when you spoke to me
The trembling sea laid bare before me
How my hand rummaged through your hair
As if searching for you when I'd never find you
And I think that if you kissed me again, I'd spend forever
Trying to find myself in your sheepish smile
Forgive me for being brash
But I think I could fall in love with you

Maybe we weren't on the same page
But I at least thought we were in the same book
Why couldn't that have been enough?

I didn't think that it would happen
In fact, I promised myself I wouldn't let it
But then you remembered things about me
A lot of things, actually
Little things, the kind of stuff that's easy to forget
But you didn't
You remembered
And then it happened
I couldn't stop it now, even if I wanted to
And what a beautifully helpless feeling it is
To feel yourself falling and not know when you'll land

I hope you never stop remembering me

The daughters of broken mothers hold their trauma close to
their chest
A scar they didn't receive but carry nonetheless
Because they know how things have gone
They have cried out and had the finger pointed back at them
from a bloody hand
They have heard the warnings and the whispers
Seen the way a woman's life can be shaped
Molded and shifted,
All without her permission
And so they do not let themselves forget the traumas of their
mothers
If only to make the world less heavy for their daughters
They remember

This house no longer suited you
So you threw a match and brought the foundation to its knees
Swept the ash into the wind
And reveled in your freedom

You rubbed salt into my wounds and told me my cries of
pain were too loud
Too distracting
Upsetting
So this was how we went on
Your action was never the issue
But my reaction was
So I learned to scream in silence
And when you held my head under water, I didn't scream
I simply waited for it to be over
And now you're gone
But I still scream into the silence
Apologize for every reaction to any negative action
I still think of you in the pockets of my day
And the tips of your fingers hold my eyelids taut
So that I can never sleep until you let me
And I have relayed the what ifs so many times that it all just
sounds the same
Because there is nothing I could have done to save you
And that is the worst part
I no longer think of how I could have saved myself
But rather if I could have pulled you from the water too

Infatuation bloomed
And suddenly we were lovers

How beautiful we could have been if the snow never came

I often say that I am lonely
And suddenly, people will emerge from the depths to tell me I am not
And they're right
Sure
I know many people
People who will tell me I am loved when I feel unlovable
People who will talk me down from the ledge
So I guess the truth is that I am lonely for you
And a million people could never change that

I locked all the doors
So you shattered the window and climbed in
Just to ask why all my doors were locked

When the liquor hits me, I am warm
And I can close my eyes and pretend you are holding me
again
Because I promised you I couldn't live without you
And I kept my word

I haven't lived a day since you left

Your skin is like ice water beneath my tongue
And when you rise to meet me,
Your aching gives way to the flood
And I am reminded of just how easily I could drown in you

I won't ask you for forever
That wouldn't be fair to you and the future isn't guaranteed
So I'll just ask you for tonight
That you'll stay will me
Wrapped up in the things we can't say but both feel
Lost in the warmth and the way your fingers glide across my skin
And if I wake up tomorrow and my head is still on your chest,
I'll ask you for tomorrow and nothing more

And if I wake up and the sheets are wrinkled and cold,
I'll know that you've made up your mind

I so desperately desire
To finally be home
To stop living in houses that have not been my own
And never will be
I am desperately seeking
To be my own
And no one else's
To be my home

Someday

I'm in love with a girl I'll never see again
She would wake up every morning and drink down the sunrise
And when she fell asleep, she always felt whole
Like tomorrow was just another chance to be wonderful
I haven't known this girl for years
But I swear I see her every night
She lives in my dreams and reminds me that I wasn't always this way
And I know I will never see her again
My first
My last
My forever love
The girl I used to be
The girl I will never be again

The girl cried wolf

And the people told her that she was wrong

That she had seen no wolf

And if she had, they asked how she had drawn the wolf to herself

Because it was easier to deny the nature of the wolf

Than to accept the truth of a girl

So when the wolf came again,

The girl did not cry

She didn't speak a word

And the wolf disappeared into the night once more

Let's talk about the weather
How you haven't seen the sun in awhile
And you've grown so used to the rain
We can talk about the snow
How it's coming quick and I don't think I'm ready for it
anymore
And we'll say that we love each other
You'll kiss me goodbye
And we'll push through the changing weather alone
Hoping we can come together next year in the sun

The children you abandoned are growing older
They're falling in love and having children you'll never know
The child you still call Jared has been Jennifer for years
And she hasn't thought of you in months
The beautiful children you adored and then discarded
They're stronger than you could ever imagine
Stronger than you
Because you weren't strong enough to love them when they bent tradition and followed their hearts
The children you left behind have moved on and grown up
But you'll hold your hate till it tears you apart
Piece
By
Piece

Sticks and stones never broke my bones
But I swear I went to pieces when you left me

I am so in love with beautiful women
The ones who laugh too loudly
The ones with their hair a mess
Who curse and make crowds fall silent with steady deep
voices
I am so in love with beautiful women
The women with so much love to give that they are bursting
at the seams
The kind of beautiful women that I wish I could be

Whenever I think that the storm has passed
I open the windows and dance in the sun
I walk on the warm cement and cherish the beauty
I sleep without restlessness
Until I wake up and the rain has come in through the windows
And the thunder is clashing without pause
And I realize the storm will never be over
And wonder if I'll continue to endure
Or succumb to the rain

We came together in the summer
Flourished in the spring
Fell apart in fall
And by the time the snow was falling
I'd forgotten the color of your eyes and how it felt to love
you

There's a woman across the aisle on the plane
A man lays his head in her lap and she plays with his hair as he sleeps
The man in front of me whispers to the woman beside him and kisses her cheek, and she smiles as she probably has a million times before
I think I've accepted many hard things in life
And I know there are people who will live their life without ever kissing their lover good morning, or knowing how it feels to come home to someone who makes them feel whole
But what a hard thing to accept that I may live this life alone
And I tell myself that I am a whole person that I am not endlessly searching for my other half
But deep down, I wonder how I will live the rest of my life
If I must live it alone
I wonder if I even can

I don't think I can

I think for you, I'll endure snoring even if it keeps me up all night
I won't complain when you use all the hot water, or forget to take out the trash
When you've had a long day at work, I think for you I'll order from the places you love even when I hate them
I think that for you, I'll hold you even when it's a million degrees and your mouth breathes in my ear
I think for you, I'd do anything and everything you could ever want or need
Because you are my everything
And I think that for you, if you'd let me,
I could be your everything too

Telling you I love you would be too hard
The words would get stuck behind my teeth and never reach
the surface
Instead, I will make sure you've eaten
I'll remind you to wear a seatbelt and drink lots of water
I'll always get you a drink when I go inside the gas station
And I hope this and more will be enough for you to
understand that I love you more than I could ever love
anyone else

I swear to fucking God, you make me feel small enough to be threaded through the eye of a needle
Like I could sew up all the things you tore apart and we could begin again
But you've cut me down so much that there isn't anything left
Yet I'm still giving you my everything
All that I am

Your fingertips have left craters on my skin
And these sheets will forever hold the impression of my white knuckled hands
I'll forever sleep on this pillow that smells of your cologne
The one I bought you before you stopped loving me
And I'm certain I'll be lying here, waiting in this bed
The mess you could not contain
Forever waiting for you to come back through my door
And remind me what it is to be whole once again

I think about my jealousy of the sun
The way it touches every part of you
Settles into crevices in depths I could never truly behold
How I long to be the bottle your lips wrap around, pull from
in desire
Or could I be the necklace that settles on your chest
Right by your heart?
To touch you would be such sweet release,
And that is all I could ever think to want

When I cut myself open, I had hoped these things inside of
me
These putrid, rotting, painful things
Would bleed from my soul and drip down the drain
But instead, I have opened myself up to even worse things
Things that are pulling me apart,
And breaking me down so that I am nothing once more

The days have begun to melt together
Aimless watercolors in endless pursuit
And the hours are ticking by slower and slower it would
seem
By now I had hoped it would stop
I didn't think this melancholy day to day could persist for
this long
But it hasn't stopped
And now I'm just wondering if I will stop first

I have not loved you for awhile

But every now and then, you slip into my mind

And a spark begins to burn

So I must stomp it out

Before it ignites

And the flames engulf me

And I am swallowed whole by the way I used to love you

To the woman I have yet to become, I am so sorry for
everything I have done
And continue to do to you
I hope you have fallen in love with yourself
That you have found peace in your own company
Perhaps by now you have found a lover, and if you have, I
hope they treat you the way you should have treated
yourself all along
And if your bed is still empty,
I just hope that you're happy
To the woman I have yet to become,
You are made of thick skin and wanderlust
Your heart has felt so much pain
And with all that you have lost
With all who you have lost
You have gone on
To the woman I have yet to become
I am proud of you
I love you
And I wish you all the best

I have grown tired
Of strong drinks and weak men
If you lack the strength to hold me up,
Then you have no place in my bed
Or my heart

Maybe you and I fell in love at the wrong time
Our paths crossed too soon at a fork in the road
And maybe you fell in love with me because you'd been
traveling too long
Because you were lonely
And I was within distance of your arm
Maybe someday you'll fall back into my lap
And I'll melt into the palm of your hand
Breathe you into me and feel whole again
But until then I'll tread down this path alone once more
With your lips remembered at the hollow of my throat

Can we mimic the sheets?
And tangle ourselves together
Become the very meaning of insatiable
Can you tell me you love me between raspy breaths?
And grasp me as if you were falling
If my skin was glass,
You'd have fogged it by now
Between your breath on my neck
And the trembling of your body
I've lost track of time
Can we mimic the sheets?
And tangle ourselves together
So we can fall in love
One
Last
Time?

I do not want to be made whole by the love of someone else
I want to be so full of my own self love
That it flows out of me
And seeps into the ground
Making the world better and more beautiful
And those around me glow
And when they're feeling low,
They may dip their cup and fill it till it overflows
I want to love myself so completely that it completes me

When it happens, you don't have to tell me
I'll know
When I wake up to the smell of coffee and you haven't
brought me a cup, I'll know
When you've stopped kissing my neck before we fall asleep
And holding my hand in the car, I'll know
And I won't be bitter, even though it will hurt
I'll simply tear my heart from my sleeve and pack it away
Kiss the door frame on my way out
And leave nothing but rumpled sheets
And the memory of stranger you used to love

We're sitting in my car bathing under red light
Your hand is on my leg
The windows are laced with frost and you're talking about something but I can't quite place my finger on what
I tell you I love you, and for the first time in forever, you say it back
Because I think we both know that tonight is the last time we will be like this
Happy
In love
Okay again
And we won't say it for fear of spoiling the moment, but sitting here under the traffic lights, I think we both know we've ran our course
And so you move your hand from my leg and I grasp it
The light turns green and we're off
Unsure of where we're going
But both knowing we won't go there together

The first time you left me, every part of my heart collapsed
And there wasn't a thing I could do without remembering
you
The second time, I barely noticed you were gone
I had to force myself to miss you just to remember your
presence
Because everything felt the same
Just easier
And that was when I knew for certain that I no longer loved
you

It's 2 am and your words are thick as you tell me you miss me

There are pauses filled with deep breathing

And I try to fill the silence with replies, but you push them back and drive on

You're telling me you love me, *you don't*

You're telling me you're sorry, *you aren't*

And I'm wondering why I'm only on your mind at times like these

When it's 2 am and no one else is awake

When you're too drunk to remember anyone's number but mine

And for the millionth time, I tell myself I won't answer when you call anymore

I'll let the ringing echo and stop

Listen to your delirious voicemails

And I'll move on

But somehow, I always end up back here

With you

At 2 am

Wondering why you can only me when you're fucked up

And why I haven't stopped loving you still

I know self-love is supposed to be
Groundbreaking
Poetic
Beautiful
It's supposed to be loving every square inch
Finding beauty in the curve of your stomach
But sometimes the hardest thing
The least beautiful thing
Is learning self-tolerance
And it is ugly
And it is painful
It is looking at your body in the mirror
At 3 am with tears streaming down your face
And begging yourself just to be okay
To accept every stretch mark
And the arms that will never be toned
Its compromise
Hoping with everything in you, that you learn not to hate
yourself
But accept
Tolerate
And sure, we can still self-love as the only true way
And yes, self-love is beautiful
But for many, and for now, self-tolerance

Self-acceptance
Is hard enough
And more than enough

It happens gradually

Just a glance becomes a stare

An interest becomes the main point of my thoughts

We're talking more, it's subtle

It happens gradually

I'm smiling at your messages, hoping you're smiling at mine

Wondering if your lips are as soft as I've imagined

It happens gradually

The first kiss is soft, something unexpected

I'm yours, your mine

Simple

I'm pulling your pillow against me when you leave in the morning, breathing in the smell of your shampoo

Planning out the day, all according to you

It happens gradually, I know the feeling

I see it happening through one-way glass, I can't stop it

It's terrifying but beautiful to be that out of control

One of us says it, the other repeats it back

We talk about the future, and our plans always involve each other

It's effortless

It happens gradually

Time goes on, the bed we used to share is rarely filled, it's often cold where you used to lay

You're coming home later and less often, and I know it's not because you've found someone else

You're just tired, tired of the arguing

We don't even yell anymore because that would require passion we've long lost

When you touch me it's out of mutual obligation, Something to convince both of us we are okay, that this is lasting and normal

When you kiss me there is no longer an explosion of color, It is all gray and lackluster

It happens gradually

I'm making dinner for two, knowing your half will just be leftovers for me tomorrow

You tell me you love me, but only when I say it first, sometimes it's just "you too"

It happens gradually

You're smiling at your phone and I'm sitting beside you

And no, I know you're not in love with someone else, not yet

But I see it happening through one-way glass

I can't stop it and I'm not sure I want to

Because seeing you smile makes me feel more than I've felt in months

And even if I'm not making you happy anymore, I'm just glad that you are

It happens suddenly

One morning you cut the cord, the same excuses I would have given you a month or so down the road

We promise we'll stay friends, and yes it hurts every part of my soul

But it's a relief knowing I don't have to carry on this charade

We can stop pretending we're okay, we can stop pretending this is viable

I pack my things, we say goodbye, and it happens gradually

I fill empty rooms with you, I sleep more than I'm awake

And I can't tell if I miss you or if I simply loathe being alone

It happens suddenly

A glance across the room, a well-placed smile

And I'm happy again

And I'm sad it's not with you, but I'm so happy to be happy again

It happens gradually

And once more I am in love

Often, self-care is just reminding myself that you don't care
And never will again

I think the worst part is that I see you everywhere

Even though I know you haven't been here for so long

If time is meant to soften my edges, to strengthen my courage, to make missing you easier, then time hasn't been made aware of her duties

Time has simply eroded the wound, exposed me more vividly

And I know that you will not come back

And they say that you're somewhere better than here

But I'm not inclined to believe you're better off, away from the ones who loved you, away from me

So if you're a believer in life after this, perhaps we'll meet again

But for now, I'll keep screaming in my head to the empty echoes that I would give anything

Anything

For you to be here again

Do you think of me?

Not just when you are lonely

Now when it is 3 am and the bed seems too cold

Not when you want someone to play with your hair

Not just when you are alone

But when it's the fourth of July

And you're watching the fireworks with a crowd of strangers

Remembering the sparks

The way skin slid across skin

The warm of your palm

Interlocked and in love

Do you remember me?

In movie theaters

Late night junk food

Drinking with your loneliness drowning you?

Do you think of me?

Do you smell my perfume and hunger for the way we used to be?

Do you miss me?

Do you still love me?

Did you ever?

If leaking faucets brewed tempests in my sink, I think I
would find it more beautiful than problematic
And maybe that is my problem
I find beauty in chaos
Broken glass on sidewalks gleams when the sun hits it
And so I have no desire to pick it up or attempt to piece
anything back together
And maybe that is my problem
I find beauty in broken beautiful things that can, and often
do hurt
I feel substance in the empty
A pulse in a dead soul
I prefer the thorns to the rose
And I have yet to love someone who doesn't hurt me
And maybe that's why I'm so broken
Because I am desperately seeking the beauty in me
But the beauty has long stopped seeking me

When the window was broken, I let in things I never intended to

When the wind drifted in, I slid under the covers but didn't touch the window

But now, time has passed

I'm picking up this broken glass alone

And it's cutting my hands and opening the soles of my feet

And still I persist

Who else would clean this glass?

Who else would fix this window but me?

Because no one else lives in this house

And it's up to me to fix it

It's up to me to maintain it

And I will not live here with this broken window any longer

I am not uncharted territory
You will not stake a flag in my heart and claim me
The stone you lay will not be the foundation to your monument of possession
You will not tell me how I must care for this land
When the ground has begun to crack
When the flowers have given way to the weeds
You will not comment on the appearance of this land
That I have so graciously allowed you to graze upon
And when you are gone, this land will go on
And you will simply be a memory in the dust long settled

New Year's resolutions often fail within a month
So these resolutions are not for the New Year, but for every
year
To fall out of love with those who cannot and will not love
me back
To fall in love with myself
Every high-pitched laugh
Every scar
Every part of me
And yes, I will better myself
But I will refuse to hate myself along the way
This year I will not hold a knife in one hand and a paint
brush in the other
I will not degrade what I long to change
I will not better myself for others to love me and respect me
the way I deserve
I will better myself for myself
I will become the kind of woman I could love
Every year, every month, every week every day every hour
every minute every second
I will love myself

It's not that you are bad for me, even though you are
It is that I am bad for myself
And I don't know how to fix that

I know this town like the palm of my hand
I can follow these roads like lines I trace across my skin
I know which places you should go and the ones you should stray from
I know who I am because I know this town
I can follow the constellations of streetlights back to the first place I broke my own heart
This town was my first love because it was all I knew
And with every painful heartbreak, I grew to know this town better
With every kiss
Every touch
Every late night spent with temporary people in this somehow permanent place
I grew
This beautifully depressing
Desperate little town
Helped mold me
Helped me grow
And no, I never bloomed
Until I enveloped my roots in better soil and a bigger vase
I know this town like the palm of my hand
But I don't think this town knows me anymore

I don't miss you

I recognize that you weren't good for me and the person I thought you were has long since left the building

But I miss someone wanting me

I miss the taste of menthol and vodka on your tongue

I miss staying up till 3 am with you and eating junk food in our bed

I miss the way you knew me

Better than I even knew myself

I miss the hunger when you pulled my lip between your teeth

The way you pulled me back into you when I pulled away in the middle of the night

I want you to know I don't miss you

I don't want you back in my heart

But I think I'd take you back in my bed

Just for a night

Oil and water were never meant to stay together
So why did we try so hard to make it work?

I remember feelings better than I ever have faces or specific times

I remember the feeling of the wind sweeping through the open window and onto my uncovered arms

How every time you spoke, my heart somehow broke and grew all at once

The way we burned through cigarettes

That menthol taste that stuck around long after you left me

And the feeling of knowing even then that you would break your promise

That I would lose myself and you because we refused to be found

How you told me you loved me at the wrong time and never truly meant it

And how fucking badly I wanted you to mean it

To say it at the right time

To not cling to those words when you left me again

And again

And again

Before life became more about getting by than the simple satisfaction I got from hearing you laugh

Now, I hear you laugh in the echoes of dreams I can't comprehend

I remember feelings better than I ever have faces or specific times
But I will never forget your face the first time I kissed you
Or the last time I felt that I could be enough
And that is why I must let you go

You look at women in passing
The bulge of their stomachs
The curve of their lips
You look at the way their thighs crash together with awe
You desire to travel the miles from tip of nose to chest
But when you look at yourself in the mirror
Sometime simply unlovable
You find it hard to fathom loving yourself the simple way
you love every woman who isn't you

I used to keep you in my pocket

And for that I am sorry

I know you wanted me to keep you in my heart

A glass of water at 3 am to quench my parched desire

But you were never my saving grace

You were a cigarette when I swore I'd quit

You were a bottle of vodka I never really wanted to drink

bit simply settled for because I had nothing else to occupy

my time

I kept you in my pocket for rainy days

Never in the sun and never when I had someone else to

placate me

And for that I am sorry

You deserved to be kept in my heart

And I am so sorry I could never love you in the fucked up

way you thought you loved me

Love without frigid undertones
Viscous like honey in tea
The soothing thing hunted for
Love truly unconditionally
Without stipulation or expectation
The way you should have loved me but never could
Is not a love I have yet found
But one my heart searches for
Like a metal detector on the beach
Just looking for a quarter
Just searching for love I should have known long ago

You keep throwing me life vests with holes in the plastic
As I drown in your water under the bridge
You tell all your friends I'm such a great swimmer
But I've been treading water since I met you
My limbs have all but forgotten how to swim
But you refuse to come and pull me to shore
Because it might just ruin your hair

We're sitting on our bed
It used to be our bed, but we won't get into that right now
We're flipping through old memories, dusting off the past
The fights
The sex
The way you used to kiss my back when you held me
How I stroked your hair until you fell asleep on my chest
And we're trying to find the crack in the foundation
The fall of our empire
The one loose brick in this house we lived in for so long that finally made the whole thing crumble when a breeze visited
But we can't
Mostly because we refuse to shine our light on the darkest corner of this cobweb ridden room
The corner where you lied to me
The corner where I sat by myself and cried over you so many times I stopped wearing mascara because all of it was wasted staining this pillow that used to smell like you before you stopped coming home
So we simply continue to sit
And page through our memories and wonder just where it all went wrong
But we both know
And we'll never say it

You spend so much time making sure glasses are full
Drinks overflowing
A desperate waitress in a rundown bar
But it's been so long since you've tasted water
Your lips turn to dust when you open them to ask for a sip

You let temptations of suicide spill from your parted lips
like a leaking bottle
To drown in the expectations that you have set for yourself
Impossible to reach
Part my lips and let me swallow the things you cannot hold
inside
We'll call it love

He told you he was an artist
And you believed him
But when he painted your skin black and blue
You became an unwilling canvas

Remember me as I was when I was happy
Don't think of me as I am now
Brash
Suicidal
With love for everyone but herself
Remember me as I was when I was happy
Or don't remember me at all

Printed in the USA
CPSIA information can be obtained
at www.ICGtesting.com
LVHW010107100823
754637LV00014B/520

9 781685 621827